MW00668697

BOOK OF EASY TROMBONE SOLOS

Edited by **Eugene Watts**
of The Canadian Brass

WITH A COMPANION CD

■

All Selections Performed by
Eugene Watts on trombone,
and pianist Patrick Hansen

■

Plus Piano Accompaniments Only

CONTENTS

In a generally progressive order of difficulty. The titles also appear in the following order on the CD.

7777 W. BLUEMOUND RD. P.O. BOX 13819 MILWAUKEE, WI 53213

WE GATHER TOGETHER

TROMBONE

Netherlands Folk Hymn
Arranged by Bill Boyd

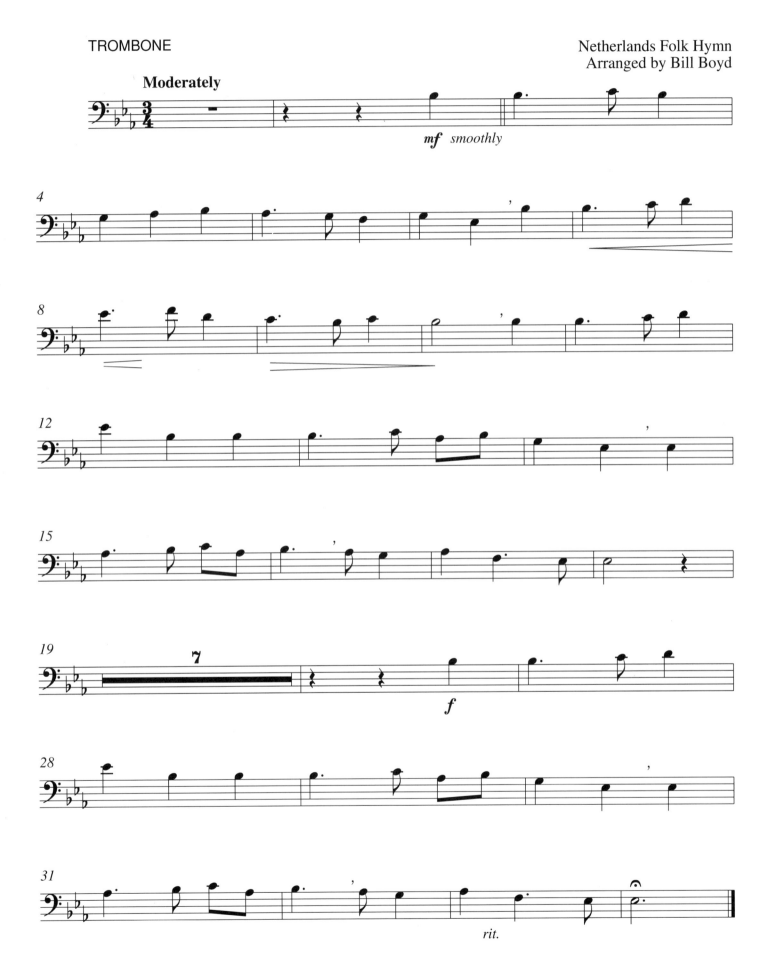

LULLABY

TROMBONE

Johannes Brahms

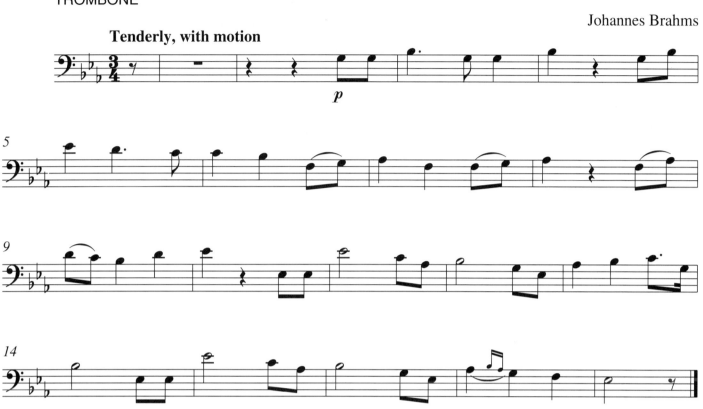

GREENSLEEVES

Old English Melody
Arranged by Bill Boyd

TROMBONE

LARGO
(Ombra mai fu)

TROMBONE

George Frideric Handel

COURT DANCE

TROMBONE

Thomas Arne

THE PLEASURES OF LOVE
(Plaisir d'amour)

TROMBONE

Jean Paul Martini

HELLO, MY BABY

Words by Ida Emerson
Music by Joseph E. Howard
Arranged by Bill Boyd

TROMBONE

EV'RY TIME I FEEL THE SPIRIT

TROMBONE

African American Spiritual
Arranged by Bill Boyd

molto rit.

LIEBESTRAUM
(A Dream of Love)

TROMBONE

Franz Liszt

CRUEL LOVE
(Sebben, crudele)

TROMBONE

Antonio Caldara

THE DRUNKEN SAILOR

Sea Chanty
Arranged by Bill Boyd

TROMBONE

BOOK OF EASY TROMBONE SOLOS

Edited by **Eugene Watts**
of The Canadian Brass

WITH A COMPANION CD

■

All Selections Performed by
Eugene Watts on trombone,
and pianist Patrick Hansen

■

Plus Piano Accompaniments Only

CONTENTS

In a generally progressive order of difficulty. The titles also appear in the following order on the CD.

The instrument pictured on the cover is a CB20 Trombone from The Canadian Brass Collection, a line of professional brass instruments marketed by The Canadian Brass.

Photo: Gordon Janowiak

7777 W. BLUEMOUND RD. P.O. BOX 13819 MILWAUKEE, WI 53213

Dear Fellow Brass Player:

We might be just a little biased, but we believe that playing a brass instrument is one of the most positive activities that anyone can pursue. Whether you're 8 years old or 60 years old, the ability to play a horn automatically creates opportunities of playing with other people in bands, orchestras and ensembles throughout your life. But to keep yourself in shape and to better your playing, it's important to regularly work at solos. You might perform a contest solo for school, or play for a church service, or just for your family in the living room. Here's a book full of solos, in varied styles, that we think you'll enjoy learning.

All this music has been recorded for you on the companion cassette. On side A each of us in The Canadian Brass has recorded all the pieces in this collection on our respective instruments, letting you hear how the music sounds. On side B you will find piano accompaniments for you to use in your practice, or if you wish, to perform with. The recordings of the solos that we have made should be used only as a guide in studying a piece. We certainly didn't go into these recording sessions with the idea of trying to create any kind of "definitive performances" of this music. There is no such thing as a definitive performance anyway. Each musician, being a unique individual, will naturally always come up with a slightly different rendition of a piece of music. We often find that students are timid about revealing their own ideas and personalities when going beyond the notes on the page in making music. After you've practiced for weeks on a piece of music, and have mastered all the technical requirements, you certainly have earned the right to play it in the way you think it sounds best! It may not be the way your friend would play it, or the way The Canadian Brass would play it. But you will have made the music your own, and that's what counts.

Good luck and Happy Brass Playing!
The Canadian Brass

EUGENE WATTS was born and raised in Sedalia, Missouri (the home of Scott Joplin). Like the story of *The Music Man,* a traveling instrument salesman convinced his parents that Gene would make a great euphonium player. He soon switched to trombone and started playing in taverns and nightclubs, steeping himself in a jazz and Dixieland tradition. He worked his way through college at the University of Missouri with his own Dixieland band, "The Missouri Mudcats." Further studies followed with Arnold Jacobs. He established an orchestral career in a succession of positions with the North Carolina, the San Antonio, and the Milwaukee Symphonies, and was asked by Seiji Ozawa to become principal trombone of the Toronto Symphony. While in Toronto, his intense interest in chamber music led to the founding of The Canadian Brass. Beyond his musical career, Gene is a continuing student of transcendental meditation.

PATRICK HANSEN, pianist, has been musical coach and assistant conductor at Des Moines Metro Opera, and has served on the staff of Juilliard Opera Center as a coach and accompanist. He was assistant editor on the new G. Schirmer Opera Anthology, and has recorded several other albums for Hal Leonard. Patrick holds degrees in piano from Simpson College and the University of Missouri at Kansas City.

WE GATHER TOGETHER

Netherlands Folk Hymn
Arranged by Bill Boyd

LULLABY

Johannes Brahms

GREENSLEEVES

Old English Melody
Arranged by Bill Boyd

LARGO
(Ombra mai fu)

George Frideric Handel

COURT DANCE

Thomas Arne

THE PLEASURES OF LOVE
(Plaisir d'amour)

Jean Paul Martini

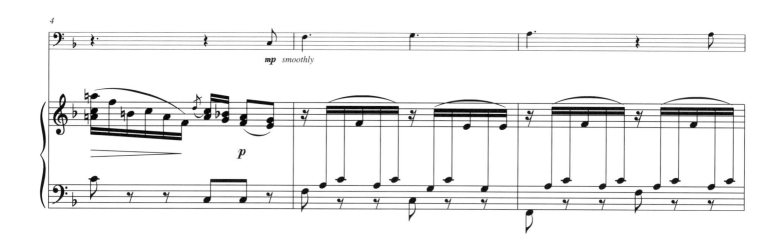

LIEBESTRAUM
(A Dream of Love)

Franz Liszt

HELLO, MY BABY

Words by Ida Emerson
Music by Joesph E. Howard
Arranged by Bill Boyd

EV'RY TIME I FEEL THE SPIRIT

African American Spiritual
Arranged by Bill Boyd

CRUEL LOVE
(Sebben, crudele)

Antonio Caldara

Allegretto grazioso

THE DRUNKEN SAILOR

Sea Chanty
Arranged by Bill Boyd